NO MOUNTAIN TOO HIGH

Written By

Rev. Dr. E.L. Smiling Jr.

Copyright © 2010 Rev. Dr. E.L. Smiling Jr.

All rights reserved. No part of this book may be reproduced in any form without written permission from the publisher and author. Except for use in any review, the reproduction or utilization of this work in whole or in part in any form by an electronic, mechanical or other means, now known or hereafter invented, including photocopying, recording, or any information storage or retrieval system, is forbidden without the written permission of the publisher and author.

K & K Houston Publishing
P.O. Box 4779
Woodbridge, VA 22194-4779
http://publishing.kkhouston.com

ISBN: 978-0-9796524-5-5

PRINTED IN THE USA

Table of Content

Introduction

I. We all have mountains in our lives
(Job 14:1)

II. Don't Let The Mountain Be A Distracter
(James 1:2-4)

III. The Word of God Can Cut Your Mountain Down
(Hebrew 4:12)

IV. Faith don't see the mountain
(Matthew 21:21)

V. Not able to do it by yourself
(John 16:7)

VI. Praise can bring the mountain down
(Joshua 6:20)

VII. Prayer sustains you during the mountain season
(Luke 18:1)

VIII. Trust God, He will see you through your mountain
(Proverb 3:5-6)

FOREWORD

As I pondered in my heart words that can be of some earthly help to someone, and being prayerful, I considered penning these words onto a manuscript, with the help and guidance of the Lord, and with much hope they might eventuate someday into a small book for someone to read and digest; here it is. The hopes also that someone might be inspired and encouraged enough to withstand the hard times and tough times encountered every day in our lives. We all face giants and mountains, but do we know how to stand when the wind blow strong? Do we know how to survive under fire? Do we know what to do when the fierce lightening begins to strike, or when the thunder roars? Do we know how to overcome our trials and tribulations and climb over Trouble Mountain? I have always wanted to write my thoughts and words of encouragement on paper, and what better way to do this than to capture the words in a book—my first book. I believe God have given me a gift to be patient enough to write words. He gave me the ability to write my thoughts and inner feelings and express them on paper. I am indeed grateful for this gift and my desire in this project is to reach as many people as possible with inspiring words that bring about a positive energy in the midst of so much turmoil. After all, there is an enormous amount of negative energy around us in the world today as we read the newspapers, and watch the news channels, and listen to news radio broadcasts, etc, etc. The thrust also in this project is to achieve a book that is not intimidating for the not so fluent and not so frequent reader.

There are many people, me included, who are simply intimidated by the size and volume of some of the books on the market today.

The idea in this project is to minimize the size and decrease so much volume so as not to be intimidating to the prospective reader. To be quite frank and to be even more specific, many in the African American and other minority communities, as well as churches, do not pick up books and just read them as a recreational pass time or as a personal hobby. Many times, in my humble opinion, the reason for this is that when they see this large book with hundreds and hundreds of pages, a little to no pictures, there is a serious level of intimidation. I don't qualify this by saying it is alright, but I am simply saying, that maybe if there is a downsizing of the volume and minimizing of the amount of pages, other, not so frequent readers may get on board.

If you need help with the mountains of life, you've picked up the right book—I urge you to read. If you need encouragement with troubles and trials in life, this is the right book—I adjure you to read it. If you feel overwhelmed with trials and with the troubles in life I assure you, this book will definitely help you with your dilemma or the many dilemmas you will face. Let me invite you to delve in and be blessed. This book is small, but I believe it can reach into places not accessible by other, larger writings to a place that needs and hunger for its content. The book is not intellectually challenging and it speaks to a universal audience who has one thing in common using three words; trouble, trial, and tribulation. You don't have to be a college graduate or own a PHD to read this book. I tried hard to make it a simple, easy to read book project. The Bible speaks of the trouble of all mankind: *"Man that is born of a woman is of few days, and full of trouble."* Job 14:1

No matter who you are or where you come from, you will have trouble. No matter what your status is in life or who you know, you will indeed have trouble. Trouble is as much a part of life as the air we breathe and need in order to survive. There is no exemption from trouble and I view trouble as being like an enormous hill or mountain that stands in our way. Trouble is like as a huge stumbling block or an oversized speed bump in our highway of life. Now it is not so much a negative thing. I tend to lend a positive thought to trouble. We need it to grow. We need it to improve character. We need mountains to help us toughen up and train ourselves on how to stand and how to overcome. Somebody once said to me, that if we never experience darkness, we will never appreciate light. Mountains are only dark places for a moment and then after we hold on and stand tall, they are eventually conquered and we experience the light. In short, mountains come, they linger for a while, and then mountains go. My aim is to help somebody while they're going through a mountainous situation.

The final touch in the writing project is to provide necessary tools a person can use to help endure the mountain season. God in His wise counsel authored a great book; the greatest book of all times; the Bible, to help us know what to do and what not to do at certain junctures in our life. In dealing with the issue of troubles, trials, and tribulations, His word is paramount. He outlines some of the tools needed; prayer, praise, bible study, trust, faith, patience, etc... He has given us everything we need to survive. It is our responsibility to pick up the bible and read it and gain the vital knowledge we so dearly need to help us through our storms. Even this book, inspired by the Holy Spirit, can give insight and help in the time of trouble. One should never, however, replace God's

Word, the Holy Bible with another book. Every other book in life is subordinate to God's Word. If we would just take the time to read it and meditate on it and ponder its precepts, and study God's Word, I promise, there will never ever be any mountain in life too high to climb or overcome. The mountain might look tall; the mountain might appear high, but it's never too high. The mountain might intimidate you at first; it might jolt you in your faith for a moment, but know it's like a lion, king of the jungle, with a loud roar, but absolutely no bite. My aim is to help you realize the magnitude of the mountain, but more so the power you possess over the mountain and the tools and equipment you possess to help you cope with the mountain and achieve utter victory over your mountain(s). Read and enjoy the book as you explore the theory and transform theory to truth about the fact that there is "No Mountain Too High."

Introduction

Mountains have always played an important part in God's dealings with His people. Look at the great mountain; Mt Sinai. When God's people left the bondage place of Egypt, they traveled for three months before arriving at Mt. Sinai. In Exodus 19:16-20:12, on this same mountain, God revealed Himself to Moses and gave him the Ten Commandments. Another great mountain in the Bible is Mt Carmel. On this mountain, Elijah challenged the false prophets of Baal and won victory over their little gods. This mountain is remembered for the miraculous showing of power of the God of Abraham, Isaac, and Jacob; read 1 Kings 18. Mt. Gerizim and Mt. Ebal are also great mountains. At the place of these two mountains, Joshua assembled all of Israel to instruct them in the Law of Moses (Joshua 8:30-35). And it was from these two mountains that God's blessings and His curses fell upon His people. And then there is Mt Nebo. Mount Nebo is the place where Moses lost his entry pass into the promise land. During this time in Bible history, God told Moses to speak to a rock and it would yield water, but He struck the rock instead (Numbers 20:8-12). As a result, He was not allowed to enter Canaan; Israel's promise land. God took him to the top of the mountain (Mt. Nebo) and afforded him the opportunity to gaze over into Canaan land, but not enter.

There are several other important mountains found in
the Bible—like the Mount of Olives (significant in that Jesus taught the disciples here, and He often prayed at this location), the mountains of Ararat (the location that Noah's ark came to rest after the Flood—Genesis 8:4), and Mt. Zion, which David took from the Jebusites (Joshua 15:63; 2 Samuel 5:7) and on which he built his palace in "the city of David." As you read in the Bible about these famous mountains, remember that God who created the mountain is not limited to just a single mountain. He can reside in the mountain, or He can be located at all of them at once; all at the same time; for He formed the mountains, and He is an omni-present

God. He's able to be everywhere at the same time.

Mountains can also have a multiplicity of meanings, and represent more than just Igneous, Sedimentary, or Metamorphic rock meshed and molten together by pressure and time. Mountains can have symbolic meaning. They can have spiritual significance beyond their physical aspects. If you live long enough, you will discover that mountains of all forms, shapes, and sizes plague the lives of the people of God. Mountains come and they go, but one thing for sure is the fact that none of them are too high to overcome and that being with divine assistance. They may look high, and appear tall; they may extend beyond the clouds and stand higher than the eyes can see, but with Jesus on your side, and with the Word of God in your heart, and with strong faith, patience, and true Godliness, we all can and we all will overcome the mountain. No mountain is too high for the people of God. No mountain can ever stand taller than God and bring defeat to the Creator of all things. The Bible declares that there's nothing too hard for God and that includes mountains.

"What is a Mountain?"

Life is full of mountains. Every person will experience or encounter a mountain or, better yet, many mountains during the span of their lifetime. Somebody may even ask the question, "What is a mountain?" Well, the dictionary defines a mountain as a land mass that projects well above its surrounding terrain; with a peak, and it is always higher than a hill. Another definition is that of a large mass of earth and rock, rising above the common level of the earth or adjacent terrain. Generally speaking, mountains are higher than 600 meters in height. Those less than 600 meters are called hills. A mountain can extend beyond the clouds. There are some that don't quite make it to the clouds but still qualifies as a mountain. Mountains can be rocky and barren. Some have trees growing on their sides and very high mountains have snow on their peaks. Believe it or not, some of the highest mountains are found at the bottom of the sea. The Hawaiian Islands are literally, the top of volcanic mountains in the Pacific Ocean. Mountains are phenomenal structures. They are wonderful and beautiful masses created on earth by God Almighty Himself. He formed and created everything, and it all belongs to Him. The Bible said, *"Before the mountains were brought forth, or ever thou hadst formed the earth and the world, even from everlasting to everlasting, thou art God." Psalm 90:2.* Jesus was found on a mountain during His temptation by satan, The Bible says, *"Again, the devil taketh him up into an exceeding high mountain, and showeth him all the kingdoms of the world, and the glory of them,"* Matthew 4:8. Mountains are plentiful throughout the Bible. We all have at some point in life, if it's on TV or in a magazine, or even reading of them in a book, we've seen or heard about mountains and we do know that mountains can be literal or they can be figurative. They can have spiritual significance, and this is what I want to target. I want to deal with the Mountain from a spiritual perspective. Now the mountain can be challenging and like as a huge obstacle, but one sure thing is the fact that no matter how high, how tough, or how tall a mountain is, with the LORD, and with Jesus on your side, you can overcome it. You can say within yourself, "with Jesus, No mountain is ever too high; with Mary's baby, No Mountain Too High, with the Rock of Ages; No Mountain Too High!

"Other meanings"

A mountain can also have other meanings. Using the term mountain can even have spiritual, symbolic, and/or figurative meaning. Many times, we use the term mountain to express a large, hard-to-overcome hurdle or obstacle in our life.

This being the case, life is full of mountains. However, even before I delve any further, I want to share with you that no matter how many are in your life or how many mountains come your way, no matter how high or how tall the mountain; with Jesus on your side you can overcome the mountain. In fact, if you have Jesus with you the victory over the mountain is already yours. Let us try to look at mountains from a spiritual perspective. When we talk about mountains, in a spiritual sense we relegate to things not in the physical, but in the spiritual realm. Mountains can be like as a stronghold that you just cannot seem to shake, and you just cannot seem to break loose from it or climb over the thing; you can't get rid of it. When referring to one's mountain from a spiritual point of view, it is not always that large rock mass or that tall elevation that extends far into the sky. A spiritual mountain can be anything that you cannot seem to defeat or overcome in life. For some of us it might be drugs. For others, it might be health issues, (i.e., cancer, diabetes, heart disease, kidney failure, cirrhosis of the liver, HIV or AIDS, etc...). Some may even struggle with anger or cigarette smoking or an overeating disorder. There are many mountains to climb, but none are ever too high; arthritis, high blood pressure, rheumatism, alcoholism, uncontrollable rage or anger, bitterness, finding a job, financial difficulty, deep in debt and can't seem to see a way out, lying, cheating, abuse, pornography, low self-esteem, depression, incarceration, trouble, trial, and tribulation, etc... The list goes on and on and there are many other figurative and spiritual meanings for the term mountain, but you need to know that no matter what kind or how high it is, how large or how wide, no matter what the mountain be, or even where the mountain lay; God is able to help you overcome that mountain. Many times, we fall in the way of trouble or better stated; trouble uninvitingly gets in our way, and it becomes a mountain of a problem. We all have mountains and high hurdles in life, but I know a man who can knock any mountain down. I know a man who can destroy a mountain or compel that mountain to move out of your way. I know a man by the name of Jesus who is able to do exceeding abundantly above all that we ask or think, according to the power that worketh in us. Jesus is able to help you overcome. Jesus said in John 16:33, *"In the world ye shall have tribulation: but be of good cheer; I have overcome the world."* And in 1 John 4:4, John records these words, *"...greater is he that is in you, than he that is in the world."* Know that you and Jesus constitute a majority over the mountain, and the world and all the mountains ever, becomes the minority. The Bible says, *"if God be for us, who or what can be against us!"* No Mountain, my friend, No Mountain my brother or my sister, No Mountain, No Mountain, No Mountain Too High!!!

I. We all have mountains in our lives

"Man that is born of a woman is of few days, and full of trouble." --Job 14:1

No one is exempt from the mountains of life.

The Bible declares in Job 14:1, *"Man that is born of a woman is of few days, and full of trouble."*

I then, declare unto you this; according to the Bible every one born into this world will indeed have his or her fair share of trouble, trial, and tribulation; and see, trouble, trial, and tribulation are all other forms of a person's mountains. Some people may have more than a fair share, or more mountains to climb than that of others, but the bottom line is all humankind encounters the mountains of life; we all have them.

I remind you again of what Jesus said in John 16:33, *"In the world ye shall have tribulation..."*

Jesus Himself informs us to ready ourselves for trial and tribulation, and ready ourselves for the mountain that stands in our way, because no man on earth is exempt.

The Bible says, *"Many are the afflictions of the righteous: but the LORD delivereth him out of them all."*-- Psalms 34:19.

It is not to one's advantage to become upset at the mountain, but to understand that we all have them, and therefore must work hard learning how to cope with them and how to overcome them. That is a part of the Christian's quest; how to deal with mountains in life. Life will throw you some of the tallest mountains ever and then sit back and see how you cope. And let me just say right now and right here, you can't cope and you can't do it buy yourself. You need Jesus!!! You need the Word of God!!!

Some men believe that once they receive Jesus as their personal Savior, then the mountains drop off and fall away. This is simply not true. You still wage mountains in your life. What Jesus does is He gives us or provides to us an alternative for dealing with our mountains. Don't ever think that because you are in church every Sunday and you read your Bible and you attend Sunday school faithfully that your mountains are dissipated or decreased. Some even believe in their heart's mind that because they pray often and have a strong relationship with Jesus, this exempt them from mountains. The fact of the matter is this, because you do these things and you have a close relationship with Jesus, your mountains are increased. The simple logic is you become a larger target in the devil's scope and sight. He strives harder to regain you as one of his again, and therefore the mountains get larger and harder to climb.

I can remember a time in my early Christian walk when I too was one to think along these lines. I somehow logically believed that if I go to church regularly, attend bible study and Sunday school, and if I accept Jesus as my savior, I would be exempt from troubles and the devises of the enemy. How wrong I was; I still experienced trouble and mountains upon mountains of tribulation, but I discovered that the more I trusted in and walked with the LORD, the better I became at dealing with these "so-called" mountains in my life. I did not become exempt; I simply became better equipped for the struggles. I became better trained on how to handle my mountains.

Now the level and scope of the mountain might be different for every Saint respectfully, but rest assured, you will have a mountain or many mountains in your life. Let me just suggest to you that you do as Paul said,

"...endure hardness, as a good soldier of Jesus Christ." --2 Timothy 2:3

And

"...run with patience the race that is set before us, looking unto Jesus the author and finisher of our faith;" --Hebrew 12:1-2.

See the race is your course of life and we all must run our race with patience, perseverance, and endurance. We've got to stay in the race and continue strong; no matter what come our way. No matter what the trial; No matter what the tribulation; Come hell or high waters, we've got to stay the course, looking unto Jesus who is the author and finisher of our faith. Then, if we keep our eyes stayed on Jesus, we can run with boldness; we can run with confidence, and we can run our God appointed race with the patience God mandates in His word for us to run.

Don't ever think you exempt from having mountains, we all have them and we'll continue having to deal with them until we die and leave this earth.

Furthermore, I believe the church and the people of God have more than the average share of mountains. We get a double dose, "if-you-will" because of our association and our relationship with Jesus.

Even Jesus had mountains to deal with. His greatest mountain was the cross. He had to endure the sentence of crucifixion and death by hanging on a rugged cross or a rugged tree, after being whipped and humiliated by the Roman authority, who put a thorny crown on his head, made Him carry the weight and burden of the cross on his weak shoulders, drove nails in his hands and feet, and administered a spear pierced wound in His side while up on a hill hanging high and stretched out wide, exploited, and hanging before the entire world to see. If Jesus had to deal with mountains, then surely you and me; we'll have to deal with them also.

II. Don't Let The Mountain Be A Distracter

The mountains in your life will distract you if you let them. It is all in the way you mentally process your mountains. You should know  that mountains are not always there as a negative force, or negative energy but sometimes they are present to test you and try your faith. Sometimes the mountain becomes a tool to make you a better person and maybe sharpen your character. In the Bible, James wrote that we should count it a joy when we experience a spiritual mountain or spiritual mountains in our life;

He wrote:

"My brethren, count it all joy when ye fall into divers temptations; Knowing this, that the trying of your faith worketh patience. But let patience have her perfect work, that ye may be perfect and entire, wanting nothing."
James 1:2-4.

Temptations also can be like as mountains in the life of a child of God. One of the implications for the word temptation as used in the above scripture text is adversity. Adversity is nothing more than hard knocks and hardships, trouble and tribulation. It's having trouble and trying times at a certain span of time in the course of one's life. Many of us cannot understand how to process joy out mountainous situations. We use the carnal eye to process the mountain and therefore, we miss the mark. Instead of using our spiritual eyes and seeing the mountain as being there for our good, and processing it as a good thing, we see it as a huge obstacle and a problem in which we have to deal with. For this reason, many are distracted by the mountain instead of seeing the mountain spiritually, as being present to help us and not do us harm. We need to understand, however, that sometimes, mountains are in our way to get us to the next level in our Christian walk. It may even be there to slow you down or stop you from heading in the wrong direction. Sometimes God uses mountains to close doors or in some cases open doors for His children. Sometimes God will allow the mountain in your life to help you with patience, or to shape your character, or He will allow the mountain in your world to make you stronger in dealing with life's storms and life's issues. The mountain can be a preparation tool. It can be a great tool to harden your soft places for a coming season of trauma and much stronger calamity. And therefore, James says count it all a joy. James wants us to rejoice and be happy about the mountains. Mountains do not always serve as negative devices. They can be helpful and thus one should never look at the mountain and be distracted by it; especially the child of God. I know the mountains can be numerous with sometimes several in your way at one time, and they can be taxing on you, but I want you to know, none of them are ever too high to climb. I know money can get funny, I know bills are due and they stack up high on your table, and it's usually more bills than income, I know trouble is in your way, and the doctor said this or he said that regarding your health, and the lawyer declared your case as too much to bear, and he dropped you like a hot potato. I know trials are stacking up in your life and you don't know which way to turn. But when the dust settles, and you come to the end of the road; understand and know that with Jesus, and by Jesus, and through Jesus, no mountain is ever too high to climb.

Mark 10:27 says,

"With men it is impossible, but not with God: for with God all things are possible."

Don't ever let mountains become a distracter. Use the mountain as a stepping stone to pedestal you to a new level in the LORD. If anything, use the mountain to gain inspiration and to gain momentum to your next level in the Kingdom. Don't let it distract you and cause you to fall out of the race. Keep the faith, and keep your head up and realize that God will never leave you, and He's promised never to forsake you and with God on your side, who can come against you as you can do all things through Christ Jesus who strengthens you!!!

III. The Word of God Can Cut Your Mountain Down

"For the word of God is quick, and powerful, and sharper than any two-edged sword..." -- Hebrews 4:12

God's Word is powerful and it cuts; it's sharp. It has enough power to cut down any mountain that is present in your life. I am a firm believer that the Word of God is the single source for the answer to all your mountains, all your problems and every issue you might have in your life. The Bible or the basic instructions before leaving earth, is that single source. It is a collection of God's instructions to man as it pertains to righteous living.

An unknown author wrote the below as it pertains to the Bible:

The Bible is a book that contains the mind of God, the state of man, the way of salvation, the doom of sinners and the happiness of believers. Its doctrines are Holy, its precepts are binding, its histories are true, and its decisions are immutable. Read it to be wise, believe it to be safe, and practice it to be Holy. It contains light to direct you, food to support you, and comfort to cheer you. It is the traveler's map, the pilgrim's staff, the pilot's compass, the soldier's sword, and the Christian's charter. Here paradise is restored, heaven opened, and the gates of Hell disclosed. Christ is its grand object, our good is its design, and the glory of God is its end. It should fill the memory, rule the heart, and guide the feet. Read it slowly, frequently, and prayerfully. It is a mine of wealth, a paradise of glory, and a river of pleasure. It is given you in life, will be opened in the judgment, and will be remembered forever. It involves the highest responsibility, will reward the greatest labor, and will condemn all who trifle with its sacred contents.

—source unknown

The Bible is the inspired Word of God, from God given to men under the unction or the anointing of the Holy Spirit. Some believe it is just another novel or just another book written by several different ordinary men, but I have found that the ultimate author of the Bible is God.

I also found that the men God used were hand-picked by God and chosen to collect His words; they were Prophets of old and men of faith whom God hand-picked to write His Words.

2 Timothy 3:16 says, *"All scripture is given by inspiration of God..."*

Because God is the inspirer, this makes the ultimate author God Himself, and He inspired these men to write His Word as He moved them to do so. Because God is the author of the book, and God is all powerful, then we should look to the Bible and God's Word (which is God Himself) for answers and instructions as to how we should handle our mountain.

This is why I confidently say that God's Word has all the answers for every mountain you might encounter in life. God's Word is a treasure of instruction and guidance. It will show you what to do, and how to do it; it will show you where to go, where not to go; it will guide you as to where to turn and where not to turn. God's Word will guide you to the utmost. It will also give you whatever is necessary for you to gain victory over your mountain.

No mountain can stand up to the awesome height and the awesome power of God's Word. The Word of God is living, its quick, its sharp, and it's powerful. It will bring down the tallest of mountains. It does not matter if it is Mt Carmel, or Mt Rushmore, Mt Saint Helen or Mt Everest. It does not matter if its trouble, trial, or any kind of tribulation in your life. Whatever the mountain might be in your life, the Word of God is able to bring it down. God's Word gives victory. And because we can go to His Word, it makes it clear that there is absolutely no mountain too high. God's Word is higher than any mountain known to man.

And some key scriptures extracted from God's Word are:

John 1:1; 14 *"In the beginning was the Word, and the Word was with God, and the Word was God...And the Word was made flesh, and dwelt among us, (and we beheld his glory, the glory as of the only begotten of the Father,) full of grace and truth."*

2 Peter 3:5-7 *"that by the Word of God the heavens were of old, and the earth standing out of the water and in the water: Whereby the world that then was, being overflowed with water, perished: But the heavens and the earth, which are now, by the same word are kept in store, reserved unto fire against the day of judgment and perdition of ungodly men."*

Psalm 119:11 *"Thy Word have I hid in mine heart, that I might not sin against thee."*

Psalm 119:105 *"Thy word is a lamp unto my feet, and a light unto my path."*

Proverbs 30:5 5 *"Every word of God is pure:"*

Matthew 4:4 *"Man shall not live by bread alone, but by every Word that proceedeth out of the mouth of God."*

John 17:17 *"Sanctify them through thy truth: thy Word is truth."*

Hebrew 11:3 *"Through faith we understand that the worlds were framed by the Word of God, so that things which are seen were not made of things which do appear."*

Psalm 119:160 *"Thy word is true from the beginning:"*

God's Word is pure, it is true, and it's powerful. It is able to sustain, save, quicken, reprove, correct, instruct, guide, and bring about victory to any person who would heed to its precepts and live by its guidance.

Because the Word of God is so strong, and so mighty, it is able to bring down all mountains that infiltrate the lives of God's people; And if you would be so bold as to enter the threshold and abide by God's Word, No mountain whatsoever will ever be too high or too hard for you to overcome. There's nothing too hard for God and no mountain too high.

No book is greater than that of the Bible; God's Word. His Word is truth and it is powerful.

The Bible teaches that

"Man shall not live by bread alone, but by every word that proceedeth out of the mouth of God." -- Matthew 4:4

The Bible is a book that feeds the spirit part of man. It is what man needs to grow spiritually. The Bible is like as fertilizer and spiritual nourishment for the spirit realm of man. As we all know, we humans need natural food to feed the body, and the body grows from natural food, but natural food does nothing for the spirit and soul entities of man. Jesus said man shall not live by bread alone. That means that natural food as well as every Word of God gives life to man.

There is a life sustaining element in the Bible. Man is composed of three parts—Body, Soul, and Spirit. The body is the outer shell of man and it gains nourishment from the physical foods we eat and digest.

The spirit is the innermost part of man and it gains nourishment and growth from a spirit source which is God—for God is a Spirit. Both of these parts constitute the outward boundary of the soul. The soul is the part of man that lives forever and it is God's desire and design that the spirit of man illuminated by and coupled with the Spirit of God governs the soul.

When a Godly illuminated spirit in man governs the soul, that person is headed in the right direction. When the soul is governed by the body or the flesh the person or the subject is lured in the wrong direction.

The Bible helps to shed light on this subject and it is God's Word that reveals the necessary light for man to travel in the right direction. We need God's word; we need the Bible. We need the book of life and Holy Bible to help guide us in the right direction. If we ignore God's Word, we have no other choice than to be led and governed by the flesh and the soul is in jeopardy of eternal damnation. This is why the Bible and God's Word is so important. It is of great import and a very necessary thing for all humanity. With God's Word to help, we can overcome the obstacles and the hills that enter our path of travel. God's Word is able to help us in overcoming our mountains, therefore, making no mountain too high to conquer. There is no mountain too high in the life of God's people or any people for that matter. No mountain too high!

IV. Faith don't see the mountain

"Jesus answered and said unto them, Verily I say unto you, If ye have faith, and doubt not, ye shall not only do this which is done to the fig tree, but also if ye shall say unto this mountain, Be thou removed, and be thou cast into the sea; it shall be done." Matt 21:21

The Bible declares that *"Faith is the substance of things hoped for and the evidence of things not seen..."* --Hebrews 11:1

It is the act of believing without seeing and knowing without having to handle a thing. Evangelical faith is to believe and trust in the promises of God.

According to Scripture, *"Abraham's faith calleth those things that be not as though they were..."* --Romans 4:17

Faith don't see "no" hill. Faith doesn't see the mountain. Faith sees over onto the other side of the mountain. The mountain might be present and right there in front of you, but strong faith looks over the mountain and around the mountain to the end result. This is why it's so important to have strong faith. Faith built up in Jesus. Faith that says, He worked it out on yesterday, I know He will work it out again.

Mountains will try your faith. Whatever the mountain is, it serves like as a measuring tool to examine you and try you in a similar fashion as that of a school kid taking a test. Mountains generally make you very

No Mountain Too High

uncomfortable and no one wants them in their life, but they're just a test. Don't cave in or give in, or give up because you're face to face with a huge mountain. When the mountain is in front of you and blocking all forward progress, it is at this time you should allow faith to come to your rescue.

Mark 11:22-23 says, *"And Jesus answering saith unto them, Have faith in God. For verily I say unto you, That whosoever shall say unto this mountain, Be thou removed, and be thou cast into the sea; and shall not doubt in his heart, but shall believe that those things which he saith shall come to pass; he shall have whatsoever he saith..."*

We can *"faith our mountains to death."* We have power in our tongue to talk to the mountains and command them to move. The Bible speaks of the power of our tongue.

Solomon wrote this fact in the book of Proverbs 18:21 *"Death and life are in the power of the tongue..."*

We have a strong weapon in our mouth. The tongue can be used to speak faith to any situation in life and command it to move out of your way.

Jesus encouraged us to *"say unto the mountain."* Talk to the mountain with unwavering faith and belief that God in you provides the power over the mountain, and

Jesus declares you shall have whatsoever you say— *"the mountain will be removed."*

When I was young in the faith and in the household of faith, I didn't really understand what it meant to speak to your situation and how you can speak it to life or you can speak it to death. I found later in my life journey, that the words we speak have power. As the proverbs mentions, that power is translated to be either life or death. Many times, we as a people bring death to our situation and cancel out victory over the situation simply because what we speak. Doubt and fear are the leading factors behind the negative words people speak when they're faced with a mountain. That's why Jesus said, "And shall not doubt in his heart"— doubt brings about the death over any chance of victory in the case of your mountain.

Another thing about faith, and what we speak it the fact that we can speak it enough until we speak it into existence;

Paul pens this faith element in Romans 4:17. This kind of faith talks about…*"calling or speaking to those things that be not, as though they were"*.

This is in direct parallel with Hebrews 11;

"Faith as being the substance of things hoped for, and the evidence of things not seen."

The idea is to speak to the mountain that stands before us with such a speech and language as though it was not present in our life. We can speak to our trouble as if we have no trouble. We can speak to financial difficulty as if we are debt free and speak financial freedom into existence. We can speak to marital problems like we don't really have a problem. Though the problem may be in your life at the moment, the idea is to speak life to that problem and it eventuates to victory. The key word is eventuates. It may take some time for the victory, but you keep speaking life and not death. Keep talking positive and not negative things to your situation. In the process of speaking life, your confidence is increases, and your doubt is decreased. You build up your belief factor through speaking life into your situation. God places emphasis on speaking to your mountain. He makes clear the fact that we should not have doubt about He being able to fix the thing, or solve the issue, or even to move the mountain; He say, "and shall not doubt in your heart". I declare unto you that if you speak to the mountain, and not doubt about God's power to remove the mountain, you will have victory. You will have success. You will achieve. You will triumph. You should never doubt, have faith and believe, and remember to speak to your mountain and Jesus declared you shall achieve victory. With faith, no mountain is ever too high to overcome. No mountain is too high for Jesus!!!

Now, one might ask how exactly does this faith come? Well, the Bible teaches that;

"Faith cometh by hearing and hearing by the Word of God." --Romans 10:17.

It is by hearing the Word of God that faith is built up and fortified in a person. I am a firm believer that the more Word you read and the more you study the Word, the stronger your faith become.

Now there are two forms of hearing when it applies to the Word of God and faith. The internal hearing when one reads the Word of God and study the Word. During the reading and study, there is an inner ear that channels that Word through the inward parts to your Spirit. Then there is the external hearing where the Word of God is heard from an external source, i.e., a preacher, a bible teacher, a radio, a TV, etc..., and that Word moves inwardly through the ear gate and enters the heart and Spiritual entities of man.

The Word of God is what backs faith. The more you hear God speak, and the louder His voice is in your inner being, the more you tend to confide in Him and believe in His power. Faith is built up by you reading and studying what God did in times past and how He performed the miraculous, time and time again, and then you measure this against your actions, your life, and personal experiences and you soon discover that God is true to His Word. He healed you when you were sick; He paid your bills when you really didn't know how your bills would get paid; He worked out the promotion for you; He granted you the new job, or the new car, or the new house; He worked on your patience and you realize over the stretch of time that you have more patience in dealing with things now, than you ever had in the past.

You read how he healed in the Bible; you read how he supplied the needs of His people, and then measure these things against how He has been blessing you and in the process of it all your faith is amplified. God has a peculiar way of speaking into your spirit until you really don't care how high or how huge the mountain is. You don't care if the mountain is physical or spiritual. You're not concerned if the mountain is drugs, or a bad economy. You're not worried about layoffs, or riffs. All you know is that God has promised to take care of you and you heard Him when said through the Apostle Paul,

"But my God shall supply all your need according to his riches in glory by Christ Jesus." --Philippians 4:19

Strong faith never looks at the mountain. It hears the Word of God through song as the songwriter states, *"He may not come when you want Him, but He'll be there right on time..."* - Tim Dilena.

You remember the Words, *"I will never leave thee, nor forsake thee."* Hebrews 13:5.

Faith doesn't see the mountain. Your faith can only hear God say the Words of Isaiah 54:17;

"No weapon that is formed against thee shall prosper."

You can hear the still small voice of His Word saying,

"With men it is impossible, but not with God: for with God all things are possible." --Mark 10:27 says.

The more you hear of God's Word, the less you see of the mountain. The Word of God builds faith.

Matthew 17:20 says, *"If ye have faith as a grain of mustard seed, ye shall say unto this mountain, Remove hence to yonder place; and it shall remove; and nothing shall be impossible unto you."*

Don't worry about that mountain; faith will look beyond the mountain and give you complete victory over the mountain.

When it's all said and done, you can say with confidence, "No Mountain Too High To Climb!"

V. Not able to do it by yourself

> *"Nevertheless, I tell you the truth; it is expedient for you that I go away: for if I go not away, the Comforter will not come unto you; but if I depart I will send him unto you."* John 16:7

You can't attack the mountain by yourself and expect victory. You need divine help.

John 16:7 says, *"Nevertheless, I tell you the truth; it is expedient for you that I go away: for if I go not away, the Comforter will not come unto you; but if I depart I will send him unto you."*

Now the Comforter in the Greek transliteration means an intercessor, an advocate, or a consoler. We call Him the Holy Ghost. In some circles, He is called the Helper. Some refer to Him as the 3rd person of the Trinity; God the Holy Spirit.

John 16:13 tells us that *"...He will guide us into all truth."* His job is to lead, guide, and direct us. He has more than one job, but this is one of His more prominent ones; to lead and guide mankind.

It is very difficult to overcome mountains in the natural, or under your own fleshly strength. We need supernatural help. That's where the Spirit of God or Holy Ghost comes into play. He is our helping power. Without God's Spirit on the inside, we are helpless and we are destined to failure. The Holy

Ghost works on our behalf. He is with us at all times. When we struggle, when we fall down – He's there to help us and pick us up and put us back on track. When we're sick He provides healing. When we're down and out, He encourages us. He's our helper. That's why it's so important for us to possess the Spirit of God in our hearts and in our lives.

I'm reminded of a story in the book of Acts, around the 19th chapter, where Paul came across certain disciples at Ephesus and asked them if or not they had received the Holy Ghost since they believed. They replied that they had not so much as heard whether there being any such Holy Ghost. They went on with a dialogue about Baptism and under whom baptism were they baptized. They replied unto John's baptism. Paul explained to them how John baptized for the remission of sin and that they should believe on Jesus who came after John. Paul expounded on the truth and after hearing this, the disciples were baptized in the name of the Lord Jesus. Paul then laid hands on the men and they received the Holy Ghost, spoke in other tongues, and prophesied as the Spirit gave them utterance.

The men in the story never knew there was such a thing as the Holy Ghost. They were operating as disciples but without the Holy Ghost. This suggests that even today, it is possible that some are operating in the Kingdom and do not possess the Holy Ghost. I believe this is one of the weaknesses of the church today. I also believe this is one of the reasons Christians cannot overcome the mountains in their lives.

Many in the church are not aware and are unlearned about the matter of the Holy Ghost. They go to church faithfully. They perform Christian duties in the church. They serve on and some even head up various ministries in the Church, but they have no Holy Ghost.

Now, we all need the Holy Ghost, especially as it pertains to mountains. You can't gain victory over your mountain without the Holy Ghost's help. When a mountain is present in your world, the Holy Ghost is your helper in dealing with the mountain. As stated earlier, the mountains in life can be a variety of things. Usually these things are problematic. They are strongholds, bondages, and burdens. They are like as trials and hard tribulations. They can be millstones, shackles, chains, yokes, and stocks in a person's life, designed to weigh a person down or hold a person captive.

Mountains can be a heavy load in your life and/or a nagging, thorny thing that makes you uncomfortable and you can't seem to shake it loose or free yourself from this thing. This is when the Holy Ghost specializes. He specializes in hard knocks and tough situations. What's bad though, is some will try to find a solution to their mountain without the help of the Holy Ghost. I've discovered that you can't buy a solution for the mountain. You can't hire a lawyer or solicit victory from a doctor. There's really no earthly resource at your disposal that can make the mountain go away or make it dissipate. The bottom line is, you need help with the mountains of life. You simply can't do it by yourself. I don't care how much money you might have in your bank account, or how important your name might be in the community you live in. I don't care who you know or how many you know. It doesn't matter what color your skin is or what your title might be. It doesn't matter if you're the president or the pope, the governor or a member of the Supreme Court. You will need help in waging the mountains of this life. You can't go at it by yourself. You need divine help, and let me suggest to you that the only real help and the only hope is God's Spirit or what we call the Holy Ghost.

"Studying the bible prepares you for the mountain"

> *"Study to show thyself approved unto God, a workman that needeth not to be ashamed, rightly dividing the word of truth." -- 2 Timothy 2:15*

Studying the Bible helps to ground a person in God's Word, and fortifies his/her faith during the mountain season. It is critical and very important that we become rooted and grounded in God's Word. When a person is grounded in God's Word, no matter how severe the storm, or how fierce the wind may blow, or how much the lightening flash, and the thunder roar, we will not be moved. Studying the Bible helps us to cope with life's issues.

"The Word of God is strong; the word of God is quick and powerful, and sharper than any two-edged sword..." --Hebrews 4:12

It was God's Word that created the mountain, so then, God's Word is also able to conquer the mountain.

By studying God's Word, it helps us to understand why the mountain exists in the first place. When we understand why a thing exists, we are able to deal with it and make better sense of the situation.

The Proverbs tells us in Proverbs 4:7,

"Wisdom is the principal thing; therefore get wisdom: and with all thy getting get understanding."

If we study and rightly divide God's Word, we begin to receive revelation as to how we should deal with the mountain. Dealing with mountains varies, because they are not the same size, shape, color, height or width. Like with anything else in life, mountains are not constant. They change and present different abstracts and therefore, we must deal with them on a case-by-case basis.

The Bible and God's Word helps us with every case we face. We simply need to study God's Word and prepare ourselves for a variety of mountains the will come our way. After we have studied and read God's Word thoroughly, and then study again and read it again, we too can share the thought—"No Mountain Too High!"

Mountains are not present in your space forever; they are there only for a season. As we read the Bible, we find in Psalm 30:5;

"weeping may endure for a night, but joy cometh in the morning."

The mountains are only there for a night season and God alone determines how long the night will be – It might be a day, or a week; it can even be an entire year or 10 years. We also find in the Bible in Isaiah 54:17;

"No weapon that is formed against thee shall prosper..."

Mountains can be like as the weapon mentioned in the scripture text. It might form up in your life and stack up against you, but rest assured, it cannot, it shall not prosper. It doesn't matter how high it stand, or how tall it peak; doesn't matter how wide or how deep; God's Word declares – It shall not prosper, it will not overtake you or defeat you. When it's all said and done, you will stand victor over the mountain. You will declare with a strong tone, "No Mountain Too High!"

Many times we read God's Word and we absorb the words at what I call face-value. That simply means we take the words and process them with an infinite intellect. Many people in our culture, in the Americas use words that may be used differently in other regions and parts of the world. As time passes, words often take on new and different meaning. It is for this reason we need to study God's Word. In the process of studying, you actually go beneath the surface meaning and you investigate things such as timeline the word or words were written, the author's cultural background and what region that author derived from; you investigate the context of his writing and ensure certain words that are similar in spelling to our western wordage, that they mean the same thing. For example, if you look at the word conversation, to many in America and western cultures, this word would mean to talk and perform a verbal exchange. To another culture or time, this same word might mean behavior and will have nothing to do with vocals or exchanging of words between two or more parties. Study helps us to interpret and analyze God's Word accurately. We study to rightly divide God's Word and when we rightly divide God's Word we ground ourselves and we come to the place where we simply move from saying to believing that there is no mountain too high.

The Psalmist declared in Psalm 34:19,

"Many are the afflictions of the righteous: but the LORD delivereth him out of them all."

Whatever the affliction, whatever the mountain might be, God said in His Word that He would deliver us from them all. In studying God's Word, I have discovered that if God said it that settles it. I remind you once again, that God created the mountains and He made the affliction, so He is more than capable of handling your mountain and making that mountain go away! God can handle any mountain, and He is able to make everything alright.

VI. Praise can bring the mountain down

"So the people shouted when the priests blew with the trumpets: and it came to pass, when the people heard the sound of the trumpet, and the people shouted with a great shout, that the wall fell down flat, so that the people went up into the city, every man straight before him, and they took the city."
--Joshua 6:20

When the mountains of life are present in your world, praise becomes paramount. Praise is a way to get heaven's attention. It also moves us closer to the Lord; as it is our purpose and duty in life to praise and glorify God.

Yesterday's Church had a saying regarding praise;

"When praises go up, blessings come down."

This saying speaks on the reciprocal principle which means if you do a thing, I will in-turn do a thing unto you. If you make a move, I will in-turn make a move. If you send it up to me, I will send it back down to you. The saying springs forth, more importantly though, from God's Word;

"Let the people praise thee, O God; let all the people praise thee. Then shall the earth yield her increase; and God, even our own God, shall bless us. God shall bless us; and all the ends of the earth shall fear him."
--Psalms 67:5-7

Praise is a powerful mechanism for the church and for the people of God. The Bible tells us that God inhabits the praises of His people – read Psalms 22:3. This really means that God dwells in praise. He lives in the praises of His people. See, one must always remember that we are God's people, the sheep of His pasture. We were created in His image. We were made to glorify him and give Him praise; for He is worthy to be praised. Praise opened the prison doors for Paul and Silas who were locked down in a Philippian jail (read Acts chapter 16). The centermost part of the Bible is praise. We often call the Psalms a collection or a book of prayer and praise and because it is in the middle and center of the Bible, we refer to it as the heart of the Bible or the heart of God. If you want to reach God's heart—start praising Him. Praise gave Jehoshaphat and the children of God victory over their enemies by setting up ambushes against themselves and the enemy destroyed each other because of the confusion brought about because God's people praised God and glorified Him before the battle—read 2 Chronicles chapter 20.

Praise brought about a great victory in this Old Testament story. And then there is the story about the walls of Jericho. Praise was vital and responsible for knocking down Jericho's walls when the children of Israel marched around the city a total of 7 days—6 days they marched and on the 7th day they marched around 7 times and made a thunderous and a loud noise of praise; Josh chapter 6. This praise was towards God and its aim was directed upward towards the God of Abraham, Isaac, and Jacob.

The Bible did say *"make a joyful noise unto the Lord, sing a new song unto Him, and Bless His holy name."*

Now we ought to know that praise helps us with mountains in that as we praise God, we remove our attention away from the mountain, per say, and we focus our sights on God. We no longer see the obstacle or the thing that hinders us or the problem that stand before us, but we see God's goodness. We see only a God who can solve all our problems. We see God as protector and provider. We see Him as the ultimate solution. Praise is mainly produced from inner thought. It is originated from deep mental ponder and meditation and when we think about God's goodness, and when we look at how He's been good to us, and how He blessed us and kept us, and how He brought us from a mighty long way, our soul simply must cry out Hallelujah. We have no choice but to shout for joy and overflow with happiness.

Praise will cut your mountain down just like it did with the walls of Jericho in the Bible. Praise has a cutting edge. It is empowered by God Himself and all of the Hosts of Heaven. Because God loves and lives in the praises of His people, praise goes to the root of the problem; roots it up and root it out. I'm a firm believer in praise.

After you have prayed and you enter into wait mode, or a state of waiting on the Lord, you can begin praising God for victory. Sometimes, it's the only thing you can do.

When the mountain is in your way, praise it down. David used praise to gain victory over the Philistine giant Goliath. He made mention that He come in the name of the LORD and that the battle is the Lord's. David gave glory to God and praised God as His deliverer. And because of His praise posture, God gave little David victory over the huge mountain of a Giant. If we praise God and give Him glory, He will give us victory. Jericho walls came down because of praise, and yours will to if you would learn to praise the name of the Lord, magnify Him, and Give Him all the glory.

VII. Prayer sustains you during the mountain season

"And he spake a parable unto them to this end, that men ought always to pray, and not to faint." --Luke 18:1

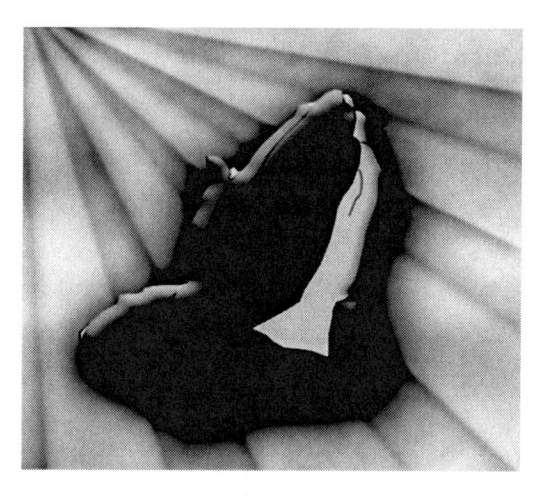

Prayer is important for the child of God. It is communication with God and Him communicating with you. Prayer is really two ways. It is the method of sending word communications upward to God who understands clearly what you are expressing to Him, and it also entails God sending a reply downward to us the receiver and we understanding his message. In prayer, there must be a sender and a receiver alternating an exchange of information; for example: Person A sends info to Person B, and Person B understands the message that Person A sent. Person B in turn sends a reply back to Person A with Person A full understanding what Person B's reply was. Many times the prayers of folk in the church are one-sided. Some pray up to God, but never receive the communication back down from God; or better stated, they don't comprehend or understand the reply from God. One of the reasons for this is people are not sensitive to the voice of God and the move of God. We simply do not spend enough time with God to understand His voice or His ways of communicating with us. Many folk do not pray enough and take time out to be quiet long enough to hear God's still, small voice. We as a people really need to slow down from the busyness of our everyday lives and things going on around us daily and listen for and learn the voice of God. Even in the midst of a traumatic situation and during the storms of life, even when mountains are present in your life, God speaks to us. He comforts us and gives us confidence and assurance that everything will be alright.

Have you ever really thought about the fact that God speaks to us? He speaks to man in many ways. For example, God uses dreams and visions; He uses other people; He uses preachers and prophets and men and women who proclaim the Gospel; He uses His Word and His Spirit; He uses children and animals; He uses trial and tribulations; He uses songs and music; He will use your enemy or your friend; He can use radio, or TV, or even the world wide web/internet, or the telephone; He even uses the mountain. God speaks to us in many ways. We just need to slow down and quiet ourselves long enough to recognize His voice and hear when He speaks.

My grandmother used to say, *"God works in mysterious ways"*, and He will sometimes use strange mechanisms to get your attention and speak to you. Look at Moses and the burning bush. God did a very strange act to get Moses' attention, and after He captured Moses' attention, then He began to speak to Moses. There's power in prayer and it is a powerful tool for the child of God. We simply must utilize prayer before, during, and after our mountain experience.

God really emphasized the medium of prayer. He was very careful in ensuring prayer was mentioned throughout the Bible. He placed heavy emphasis on prayer. Prophets of the Old Testament and the new prayed often. This was their means of comfort and sustainment during trying times. They also, on occasion, wanted protection and deliverance from enemy forces that came against them. Prayer brings about peace and tranquility, and a kind of ease of spirit when things around you are turned upside down or inside out. Prayer gives you a kind of spiritual strength to stand firm and not waiver during the storms of life and again, the mountains in your life are symbolic to the storms in your life; the two are symbolic, but also equal.

Mountains have a way of knocking us to our knees. This is really one of the beauties of the mountain. It keeps us humble. It keeps us in a prayer posture. The higher the mountain, the more we're apt to pray.

The apostle Paul put it this way, *"Pray without ceasing"* 1 Thessalonians 5:17.

He intimates to the church that we should always be found with prayer in mind, in heart and in mouth. Under the unction of the Holy Spirit, the suggestion is that we should always have God on the brain.

Colossians 3:2 tells us to *"Set your affection on things above, not on things on the earth."*

It directs us to set our minds and hearts on God above; on heavenly things and not things down here on the earth. What a mighty God we serve. This sounds like an almost impossible task, however, its not. When the mountains are present; and I say mountains because sometimes there are more than one mountain at a time present in your life, it is at this time we can exercise prayer, by setting our attention on God above, rather than looking at that mountain.

When the burdens of life come and occupy your world with troubles, problems, issues, tribulations, etc..., you need to start praying. Even when things are going well in your life, you ought to pray. One songwriter said, Prayer is the Key... and a key unlocks doors. In other words, prayer is the key to bringing down any mountain that may be present in your life.

Many prayed in times past. Abraham prayed unto God: and God healed Abimelech, and his wife, and his maidservants; and they bear children in Genesis 20:17. Daniel prayed 3 times a day.

The Bible said, *"he kneeled upon his knees three times a day, and prayed, and gave thanks before his God..."* --Daniel 6:10

Jabez prayed to God, the familiar prayer of Jabez; And God granted him that which he requested. Elijah prayed under a Juniper tree that the Lord would take his life; but God restored him with bread and water. In 1 Kings 19:4 David prayed and sung Psalms unto the LORD. He wrote much of the book of Psalms. Jonah prayed unto the LORD his God out of the fish's belly in Jonah 2:1. Prayer was made without ceasing of the church unto God for Peter, who was kept in prison. As a result of the church praying, Peter was freed from captivity. Prayer is a powerful benefit for the Saint. God wants us to pray. Peter even picked it up and under the inspiration of the Holy Ghost,

>He said, *"Pray without ceasing."*
>--1 Thessalonians 5:17

Prayer will turn your life around. Prayer will set you free. Prayer will fix whatever is broken. Prayer will heal your sickness. It will lighten your load and ease your heavy burden. Prayer is a must. Every child of God "otta" pray always and in everything. Send up some timber as the old folks used to say.

Send up some timber and watch God move in the earth. When you pray be effectual, and be fervent as the Bible declares,

"The effectual fervent prayer of a righteous man availeth much." James 5:16.

Pray in the morning; pray in the noon day; pray in the evening hour, and pray late in the midnight hour. But whatever you do, don't ever forget to pray and talk to God frequently. One song writer wrote,

"Have a little talk with Jesus, tell Him all about your troubles, He'll hear your faintest cry, and He'll answer by and by."

When you come face to face with this tall mountain and when you're at the base of your trouble and you have to look up because the mountain is so tall in front of you and the trouble is so hard, don't forget to pray. Since you're already looking up, do like the Psalmist said in Psalms 121:1-2;

"I will lift up mine eyes unto the hills, from whence cometh my help; my help cometh from the LORD, which made heaven and earth."

Prayer changed things and it will turn your situation completely around.

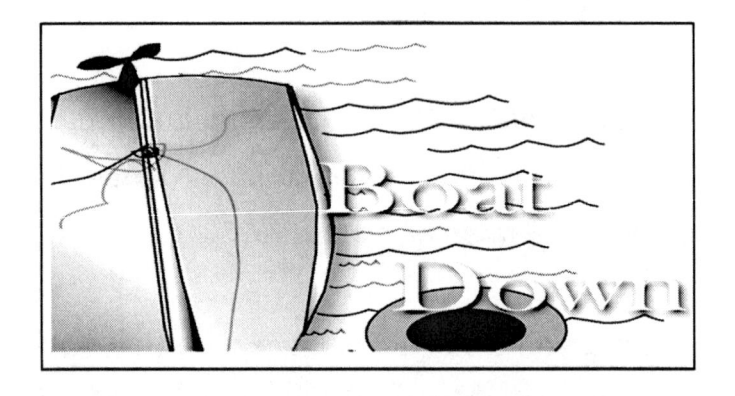

Boat Down

I am a living witness to the power of prayer. I can remember when I was in a serious boating accident some 12 years ago. While I was home for a brief visit, my father, my brother and I, decided to go boating in a local river. The small vessel we were cruising in capsized while we were drifting slowly through this large river system, down in the thick, muddy waters of Black River located in central South Carolina. We had cruised about 5 to 7 miles from our docking point and it was during the evening hours of the day.

There was a mild overcast and rain was in the near forecast. The idea was to go for a short cruise and return before the heavy rainfall. What started out to be a brief boat ride became quite an elongated journey. This accident became a huge turning point in my life as this was one of the many mountains that I had to deal with and one I will forever appreciate. I can remember the water as being rapid moving water with strong current flow. I knew of the LORD, but had strayed away from the faith and had been that way for many years. It all happened so fast. I was at the helm.

We made a pit stop along a small shoreline to use nature's bathroom. When we returned to the vessel, I launched away from the shoreline with a too sharp of a turn and with too much acceleration. With the rear motor end of the vessel already being low to the water surface, this caused that end of the boat to dip too low into the water. Not noticing this in time, the water began to overcome the lower back end of the vessel and by the time it was noticed the small vessel could not be recovered. It slowly became full of water and toppled over "bottoms up". Everything and everyone in the vessel was poured into the river, we included. This became the beginning of a mountain in my life I would never forget. I began to pray.

Thanks be to God that we all knew how to swim. The water current was not as strong in the area we went down in as it was in other places and we all were able to come back quickly to the surface. It was a little scary for my brother though.

My father and I came straight up and were able to find refuge on the upside-down boat which was caught up on a tree limb or something underneath the water. We, however, could not find my brother. He had not come up as fast as we did. So I began to pray. I asked God to please do not let my little brother die in the river that day. After a short while, he pops up about 25 yards away standing straight up in the water— Prayer works my friend; praise the name of the LORD. He was standing on a huge tree limb that had fallen into the water and because the river was so deep the tree and/or the branch from the tree was under the water surface and it appeared that Anthony was standing suspended atop the water, "walking on water" if you will.

This was only the beginning. The river width where we landed was approximately 50 to 70 yards wide and we were stuck somewhere about mid-way. We needed to make a decision to go to either of the two shorelines. The vehicle side of the river, which was 5 to 7 miles away, was the side we really wanted to swim to, but after making many turns and maneuvering forks and branches in the stream, we soon dismissed that idea and decided to go to the shorter of the two sides. When we made it, we discovered the foliage atop the shore banks were too heavy for us to travel in and navigate, and the best solution was to stay in the water as this way we could make better time towards our vehicle.

We realized that there was not many fishermen left as the rain had begun to fall and the sun was beginning to set. We were in a tough place. We were in a river, during night hours, at the mercy of the wild predatory animals as well as trying to move about in waters with strong undercurrents. I can remember constantly praying and talking to God and pleading with Him that neither of us, especially my father and brother, would be lost in this experience. I prayed all the night long and continued to pray. I lost my glasses and could not see anything except the white shirt my father was wearing, but this allowed me to look more to God than to my surroundings.

This was a huge mountain for me, and I don't think I could have made it without the medium of prayer. So, when morning finally came and to make a long story short, we were spotted by an angler who was on an early morning excursion cruising along the river. He made mention that he saw the capsized vessel upstream and knew that someone was possibly stranded along the river. He also made mention that his experience with this river was that it is swamped with gators and large predatory wildlife and that we were "lucky" to have survived during the night hours treading water. My reply to this was, "It was the power of prayer". God heard the prayers and He smiled on us. And I declare unto all this day, that prayer will diminish your mountain. Prayer will kill your mountain. Prayer will destroy your mountain. And I hold to my firm conviction that prayer is a weapon against any mountain you might have and you "otta" know that there's "No Mountain Too High!" "Not one; No, not one, No Mountain is ever Too High for prayer."

VIII. Trust God, He will see you through your mountain

Trust in the LORD with all thine heart; and lean not unto thine own understanding. In all thy ways acknowledge him, and he shall direct thy paths. Proverb 3:5-6

While the mountain is present; God wants us to trust Him and trust Him alone to help us when we come face-to-face with an overwhelming mountain. The Bible says *"He is a very present help in the time of trouble..."* Psalms 46:1. He's a very present help. He's help right now. You don't have to call 911. You don't have to call the Sheriff's office. You don't need to call the fire station or first responders or the medical emergency hotline. All you need do is put your total trust in God. All you've got to do is simply trust in God. We cannot overcome our mountain if we never trust and believe that God will help see us through it. Somewhere along the line, you've got to just trust and believe that God is able, and that you're going to just trust in Him for the solution and answer for your situation.

Trust requires that you turn it loose and allow God to grab hold of it. God can't help you with the thing if you won't let go of the other end. As long as you hold on to it or even a portion of it, God will not be able to completely acquit or exonerate you of this thing. Turn it loose; let go of it, and give it over to God. Give your burden to Jesus and He will in-turn work it out.

Trust is belief and confidence in God that He's able to see you through any difficult situation; no limitations. Trust is resting in the fact that God is able to handle all things. It's having inner assurance that He will not fail you; He'll never leave you hanging; He'll never leave you alone. God will see you through your mountain. He's just asking that you trust Him. Put your trust in God alone and don't waver—just trust in Him. I promise you, He won't let you down. Man might fail you; your friend might leave you hanging; your family might turn their back on you; Church folk might not be available; Momma might be too old to help, or Daddy may be a bit too feeble; but you otta know, that God is able and He will help you and assist you in getting through your mountain experience. We've gotta learn to trust in God and surrender all your cares or better yet, cast all your cares on Him—He will see you through!

Sometimes our trust and belief factor becomes weak and a bit shaky. There are times when the mountain seems so high and so large until we feel intimidated. We become fearful and affrighted by the size of the dilemma. We allow fear to cause us to doubt God and we become unstable in our faith. Fear is not of God.

The Bible says, *"For God hath not given us the spirit of fear; but of power, and of love, and of a sound mind."* --2 Timothy 1:7.

We should never let fear, "an ungodly spirit", get in the way of totally trusting and believing that God is able. We should push fear aside by using what I call self-encouragement tactics. The Bible teaches in principle that God is light and the devil and evil is darkness. The light and darkness cannot occupy the same space. When light enters a dark space, the light overwhelms the space and darkness dissipates. So in keeping with this principle, fear is not of God; it is darkness and it represents a spirit from the devil which is directly opposite God who is light.

1 John 1:5 says, *"God is light, and in him is no darkness at all."*

So then, God is light and the devil is darkness. Since fear is of the devil and it represents darkness and we know that God is light, we can bring or speak God's Word in light of the fear and cause darkness to flee.

James 4:7 says, *"Submit yourselves therefore to God. Resist the devil, and he will flee from you."*

We don't have to allow fear to get the best of us and cause us to waiver in our faith. Encourage yourself by using God's Word. Begin to speak to yourself about how God said in His Word,

"I will never leave thee, nor forsake thee." Hebrew 13:5.

How Jeremiah said, *"Ah Lord GOD! Behold, thou hast made the heaven and the earth by thy great power and stretched out arm, and there is nothing **too hard** for thee:"* Jeremiah 32:17.

You can encourage yourself with the Light of God's Word.

He said in Rom 8:28, *"And we know that all things work together for good to them that love God, to them who are the called according to his purpose."*

And look at the Hebrew boys in Dan 3:17, they said, *"If it is so, our God whom we serve **is able** to deliver us from the burning fiery furnace, and he will deliver us out of thine hand, O king."*

These are just a few extracts of God's Word that you can use to encourage yourself and bring light to what appears to be a dark situation. And when you remove the darkness and the doubt, then and only then can you really begin to trust and believe that God can do anything. He can do anything but fail.

Proverbs 3:5-6 says, *"Trust in the LORD with all thine heart; and lean not unto thine own understanding. In all thy ways acknowledge him, and he shall direct thy paths."*

God, through the wisdom of King David's son Solomon instructs us to Trust in the LORD. He wants us to rely on Him and release our cares and concerns over to Him who is able to handle all earthly issues.

My mother used to say, *"Earth have no sickness, Heaven cannot heal."* I took it a little further and said, *"Earth has no problems, Heaven cannot solve."*

Our part in this is to turn things over to God and as He told the Israelites at the edge of the Red Sea, in Exodus 14:13,

"Fear ye not, stand still, and see the salvation of the LORD, which he will show to you today: for the Egyptians whom ye have seen today, ye shall see them again no more forever."

Israel was in a tight spot and they were facing a dilemma. After Pharaoh had freed them and they were well into the desert and had arrived at the mouth of the Red Sea, they noticed old Pharaoh and his army were in pursue of them as if to siege them and bring them back into bondage. The children of Israel became fearful and afraid. They began to break down and break away from the faith. They had forgotten how to trust in the LORD. They forgot how to surrender all to the God of all. They did not remember how to totally give all their cares and concerns, issues and problems to a God who was able to set them at liberty from the strong arm of Egypt. Moses therefore took to remind them that God is still God and He's still able to do all things, and all power is still in His hands. So Moses encouraged them to stand still, be quiet, don't waiver, don't flip out, don't trip, stand still and see for yourselves how God is about to deliver. Stand still and see God do what He said he'd do. They simply needed to trust in the LORD give all their worries to the God of Abraham, Isaac, and Jacob. And that's what we all need to do, we need to trust in God and turn all our problems over to Him. He's able to handle your mountain. He's able to manage your mountain. He's even able to move your mountain and inspire you to the place that you realize there's no mountain too high.

We must know that God is above all our mountains. We simply need to understand that God is maker of the mountain; He's maker and sustainer of all things. God is author and finisher; He's top dog as it applies to creation. No mountain is ever too hard for God to handle. Think about your mountain even now. If you have a mountain, God can bring it down. God can cut the mountain down to the ground, but you have to trust Him and He will do the rest. He will take care of your situation and He will work it out. Trust in the LORD and He will tame your mountain.

CONCLUSION

Mountains have always been around and they will continue to be around. As long as we are alive in this world, we will have mountains. They are tailored and designed and customized just for you by God Himself. What an awesome thought! What an awesome imagery. Something customized by God, just for you and just for me. I feel exhilarated knowing God have me in mind. Mountains are never designed to harm you or hurt you in any way. They are designed to sharpen you and better you in the place of your character. They are designed to make you stronger and build you up so that you can withstand the wiles of the enemy and the trials and tribulations that cometh your way. In a way, we need the mountain. We need the testing and the trials that we are presented with. I like to make the analogy like this, if it never rain and become cloudy, we will never appreciate the sunshine on a clear day. After being rainy, windy, stormy, and cloudy for a while, you tend to appreciate the clear and sun shining day when it arrives. Mountains are not a bad thing. God allow them in our lives to try our faith and test us to better us. The mountains can represent many things in life, e.g. financial hardship, marital problems, drugs, alcohol, cigarettes, sickness, foreclosure, auto repossession, problems with children, legal problems, homelessness, imprisonment, sin and guilt, immorality, infidelity, etc... The mountain can range from a single issue, to a combination of many problems at the same time. In some churches we simply call it "going through" or "the storms of life." Some say, "I'm going through a storm". There are a plethora of things in life that qualify as a mountain. The mountains might be present, but God is bigger than the mountain. The encouragement is to know that no mountain is ever too big or too high for God. God made the mountain, and God can surely move the mountain.

We ought to embrace our mountains as James wrote in James 1:1-4,

"count it all joy when ye fall into divers temptations; Knowing this, that the trying of your faith worketh patience. But let patience have her perfect work, that ye may be perfect and entire, wanting nothing..."

We ought to rejoice when we get them, for they work our patience which perfects us in the department of patience; and we all can use work in that department; leaving us perfect and complete and in want for and in lack of nothing. The attitude about the mountain ought to be Hallelujah and thank you Jesus! We ought to shout and praise God when they come our way. The troubles of life suggest that you're being considered for a blessing. It's like as a person in training or in a school environment preparing for a final test and the day of testing is upon him/her. This test is the final exam before the completion and certification; before the reward is achieved. The reward is not obtained until the test is administered and passed. The test becomes an opportunity for the victory. When we are faced with mountains, it only means we now have an opportunity for victory, so we should rejoice.

Romans 8:37 assures us that we have the victory; it says, *"Nay, in all these things we are more than conquerors through him that loved us."*

Knowing this, we already know the outcome of the mountain is victory because the Bible tells us,

"... thanks be to God, which giveth us the victory through our Lord Jesus Christ." 1 Corinthians 15:57.

When your mountain comes, "Shout!" When your mountain shows up, "Rejoice!" When your mountain appears, give God the "Praise!" It is at this time that you're being considered for a blessing. And again my friend, it is my strong conviction and I want to share with you the fact that there is absolutely no mountain too high; absolutely none! No not one.

The mountain is not the end of the world. The mountain is not the end of your life. In my opinion the mountain is not even a permanent thing. It is temporal and it is only for a season. Mountains come and mountains go.

There are many ways to deal with the mountains when they are present in your life. Faith over your mountain, the Holy Spirit to help us climb and overcome our mountain, praise for victory over the mountain, prayer, and trust in God are a few means for which we are given to help us cope with our mountain. These things also help us overcome the mountains of life. There may be times you need to draw from God's Word. His Word is the prime source to help us when we need victory over any mountain.

The Word of God has a remedy and a solution, as well as a fix, for anything that life might sling your way. You simply should never try to deal with a mountain without going to God's Word. That's why some describe the Bible as basic instructions before leaving earth.

There is Godly instruction, inspiration, hope, encouragement, enlightenment, and everything you need all stored up in God's Word. As I walk closer to God, my perspective has evolved into one that clearly sees that there really is no mountain too high. God is the highest and there's simply nothing higher than God. Be encouraged and know my brothers and my sisters in Christ; that there's absolutely no mountain ever too high!!! God Bless and Amen!!!

Notes

Notes

Notes